Date: 02/02/12

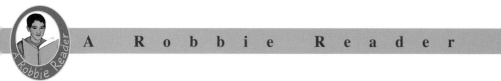

How To Convince Your Parents You Can...

Care For A Kitten

Stephanie Bearce

Mitchell Lane

PUBLISHERS

P.O. Box 196
Hockessin, Delaware 19707
Visit us on the web: www.mitchelllane.com
Comments? email us: mitchelllane@mitchelllane.com

Mitchell Lane
PUBLISHERS

Printing   2   3   4   5   6   7   8   9

A Robbie Reader/How to Convince Your Parents You Can...

Care for a Kitten	Care for a Pet Mouse
Care for a Pet Bunny	Care for a Pet Parrot
Care for a Pet Chameleon	Care for a Pet Racing Pigeon
Care for a Pet Chimpanzee	Care for a Pet Snake
Care for a Pet Chinchilla	Care for a Pet Sugar Glider
Care for a Pet Ferret	Care for a Pet Tarantula
Care for a Pet Guinea Pig	Care for a Pet Wolfdog
Care for a Pet Hamster	Care for a Potbellied Pig
Care for a Pet Hedgehog	Care for a Puppy
Care for a Pet Horse	Care for a Wild Chincoteague Pony

Library of Congress Cataloging-in-Publication Data
Bearce, Stephanie.
  Care for a kitten / by Stephanie Bearce.
    p. cm. — (A Robbie reader. How to convince your parents you can—)
  Includes bibliographical references and index.
  ISBN 978-1-58415-803-5 (library bound)
  1. Kittens—Juvenile literature. I. Title. II. Title: How to convince your parents you can—care for a kitten.
  SF445.7.B385 2010
  636.8'07—dc22

2009027352

ABOUT THE AUTHOR: Stephanie Bearce is a science teacher from Missouri. She has written several books for Mitchell Lane Publishers, including *All About Electric and Hybrid Cars and Who's Driving Them* and *A Kid's Guide to Container Gardening.* Stephanie has always loved playing with kittens and has two of her own.

PUBLISHER'S NOTE: The facts on which this story is based have been thoroughly researched. Documentation of such research is listed on page 30. While every possible effort has been made to ensure accuracy, the publisher will not assume liability for damages caused by inaccuracies in the data, and makes no warranty on the accuracy of the information contained herein.

PLB

TABLE OF CONTENTS

Words in bold type can be found in the glossary.

Kittens learn to be friends with people through petting and holding. The more you play with your kitten, the friendlier it will be.

A FURRY FRIEND

Would you like a furry pet that likes to jump, play, cuddle, and **purr**? If so, a **kitten** could be the perfect pet for you. Baby cats are called kittens, and they like to be with people. They enjoy playing games, chasing string, and batting balls with their paws. Kittens love sitting on a person's lap and being petted. They are small and like to live inside with people. Kittens make great pets.

Have your parents said that a pet would be too messy in the house? Kittens are neat and tidy animals. They do not often need a bath because they use their tongue and paws to clean their fur. Kittens are also tidy about their bathroom habits and quickly learn to use a **litter box**.

Do your parents say that a pet needs lots of room? Are they worried about exercising a pet? You can tell them that kittens do not need a lot of space.

A scratching post with platforms allows kittens to climb and safely sharpen their claws. While some owners choose to declaw their animals, others consider declawing to be cruel. Instead of declawing, some pet owners apply claw covers such as Soft Paws.

They are happy living in small apartments and are good pets for people who live in towns and cities. Kittens do not need to go to the park for exercise, and they do not need to be walked on a leash. They exercise by jumping and running around the house. Because they are so active, it is important to keep their play space clean and free from objects that could hurt them. Kittens must be supervised to ensure they don't tear up things they shouldn't—like furniture, carpets, or curtains.

fun**FACTS**

The world's biggest cat weighed 47 pounds. The record for the smallest cat is one and a half pounds. Most cats weigh about 12 pounds.

Do your parents think it costs too much for a pet? You can tell them that kittens are not too expensive. You can adopt kittens from animal shelters, or you can look in the newspaper to find people who are giving away kittens for free. Kittens do not need lots of expensive food. Most kittens like to eat dry cat food. They only need about a cup of food a day. Kittens do need regular visits to the **veterinarian** (veh-truh-NAYR-ee-un). Every year your kitten will need shots to keep him or her healthy. This can cost over $100. Sometimes kittens can become ill, and they may need medicine from a veterinarian. This is another cost of having a kitten for a pet.

When kittens are happy they will purr. Purring is a deep rumbling sound in the kitten's chest. It is fun to pet a kitten and make it purr.

Petting a kitten can also make you feel better when you have had a bad day. Doctors have found that when people sit quietly and pet a kitten, their hearts beat slower. That makes their blood pressure lower, and low blood pressure is a good thing. You can tell your family that having a kitten will be good for their health.

Kittens are fun to watch. They are great athletes. This is because they have a good sense of balance. If they jump or fall, they usually land on their feet. They have special muscles that help them twist their bodies in the air. Kittens have strong leg muscles. They learn to climb and jump when they are very young.

Kittens are naturally playful and love to pounce and wrestle with other cats. Some owners do not allow their kittens outside. Cats are natural **predators**, and are known to hunt songbirds. Keeping your kitten inside will also keep your pet safe.

Kittens are smart and love to learn. Sometimes people think that you cannot teach a kitten tricks. That is because kittens are **independent** (in-dee-PEN-dunt). They like to explore on their own and do what they want. But kittens can learn rules and how to obey. You can teach your kitten to come and sit, to lie down, and maybe even how to ring doorbells and flush toilets.

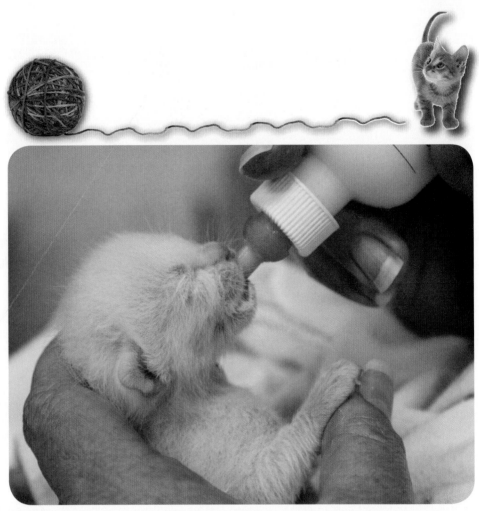

Kittens cannot see or hear when they are born. They use their sense of touch and smell to identify their mother and siblings.

ALL ABOUT KITTENS

People have had kittens as pets for hundreds of years. The ancient Egyptians had cats and kittens that guarded their grain. Rats and mice were a terrible problem for the Egyptians. The rats would eat the grain that people needed for food. The Egyptian people liked kittens because they would chase the rats. They loved the kittens so much that they became pets. There are pictures in pyramids of kittens living in Egyptian homes.

Today, kittens are some of the most popular pets in the world. You can find them in apartments in New York City. You can see them in Paris, France, or on farms in Missouri. Almost anywhere there are people, you will find kittens.

Your pet kitten has some interesting **feline** (FEE-lyn) relatives. Felines are members of the cat family. Other felines are lions, tigers, and cheetahs. All of

these animals are **mammals**. Mammals have fur or hair, and they feed their babies milk.

When kittens are born, they are small and helpless. They weigh only four ounces, and they cannot walk or see. They depend on their mothers to feed and clean them. At three weeks, a kitten's eyes will be developed enough that they can see and recognize their mother. It takes nearly ten weeks for their eyes to be fully developed. Kittens learn to walk when they are three to four weeks old. At twelve weeks old they can run, play, and drink from a bowl. That's when a kitten is ready to leave its mother and join its new family.

fun**FACTS**

Ancient Egyptians loved their kittens. They shaved their eyebrows when a kitten died. They made kitten mummies. A person who killed a kitten could be arrested.

Cats are **nocturnal** (nok-TUR-nul), meaning they sleep during the day and play and hunt at night. Your kitten will sleep while you are at school. It will be ready to play when you get home.

Nocturnal animals have special eyes that help them see in the dark. Their eyes let in more light than

Kittens need to be with their mothers until they are 12 weeks old in order to learn all their social skills.

A kitten must be able to eat on its own before it is ready for its new home.

An Egyptian painting (above) from the Deir el Medina tomb shows two cats as part of the family. The oldest picture of a cat was found in the tomb of Baket III. It is almost 5,000 years old and shows a cat hunting a rat.

Cats were so loved in ancient Egypt that some people worshiped them as gods. Bastet (left) was the name of the cat goddess. There were many statues and pictures created in her honor.

human eyes. Look at a picture of the eyes of a kitten. Look at your eyes in a mirror. Can you see the difference? Your eyes have round **pupils** (the black part of the eye). Kitten's eyes have a different pupil. It looks like a black line. When it gets dark, the pupil gets bigger to let more light into the eye. This helps it see in the dark.

Kittens also have **whiskers**. The whiskers are long pieces of hair on the kitten's face. They help the kitten to feel in the dark. If a space is too small for the kitten to fit, the kitten can feel that with its whiskers. The kitten will know not to crawl in that space.

Kittens have **retractable claws** on their feet. That means they can push their claws out or pull them in. Kittens use their claws to climb, and as protection. If something scares or hurts it, a kitten will scratch with its claws.

The tail of a kitten is also important. It helps a kitten balance. Kittens communicate (kuh-MYOO-nuh-kayt) with their tails. You can look at a kitten's tail and learn how it feels. If the tail is straight up, the kitten is interested in something. If the tail is down low and puffed out, the kitten is scared. If the tail is moving fast, the kitten is mad. You can learn a lot about your kitten just by watching its tail.

Tabby cats have stripes, spots, or whorls on their fur. Tabbies can be orange, brown, or gray. They all have stripes that make an M over their eyes.

Chapter Three

CHOOSING A KITTEN

Picking out a kitten is exciting. You will be meeting a new friend. Kittens are all different. Some are shy and quiet. Others are playful or cuddly. They can be striped, spotted, fluffy, or sleek. If you can convince your parents, one of those kittens will be your pet.

First you must decide where to get your kitten. Animal shelters are a good place to look. Kittens in shelters do not have a home of their own. They are waiting to be adopted. You will need your parent's or parents' permission, and your family will have to fill out some papers. In the papers you will promise to give your kitten a safe home and take care of the kitten's medical needs.

Some places will charge a fee for a kitten, but it is usually not too expensive. The fee pays for shots that prevent diseases. It also pays for **spaying** or **neutering**. These operations will keep your kitten from having babies. This is a good idea. It helps keep down the number of homeless kittens in the world. Your family will enjoy one kitten. They will not want ten kittens.

You can also find free kittens in newspaper ads. However, these kittens will still need shots, and you'll have to get those from the veterinarian.

When you pick your kitten, you need to make sure it is healthy. Look at the kitten's eyes. Check to see that they are clear and don't have any sticky or gooey liquid. The gooey liquid means it has an **infection** and will need medicine.

Check the kitten's ears. They should be clean and should not smell bad. A smelly ear means it is infected. Pick a kitten with good clean ears.

*fun*FACTS

Kittens have more than 20 muscles in each ear. They can move one ear in one direction and the other ear in another. Their ears rotate like radar dishes to find where a sound is coming from.

Look at the kitten's fur. It should be clean and it should smell good. Look closely to see if the kitten has fleas. Fleas are tiny insects that bite kittens. They can get in your house and in your carpet. Fleas bite people, too. If your kitten has fleas, it will need to be

All kittens are born with blue eyes. At four weeks the kittens' eyes will develop their adult color. Cats' eyes can be green, brown, gold, or blue.

treated with a special type of shampoo. If fleas get in your house, you will need to hire an exterminator (ek-STER-mih-nay-tur). An exterminator is a person who sprays for bugs. It can be very expensive to get rid of fleas.

You should also check your kitten's feet, legs, and tail. Make sure the kitten can walk easily and there are no sores.

If you take good care of your kitten, it will be your friend for many years. Kittens can live to be 20 years old. A few cats have lived to be 30 years old. The world's oldest cat was 36 years old.

Kittens come in different colors and types of fur. Persians and Himalayans have long hair. The American shorthair and the Abyssinian are short-haired. Most cats are mixed breed, but some cats are purebred. Purebred cats have the same traits (color, size, shape, and sometimes personality) as other cats in its breed.

fun FACTS

Most kittens have five toes on each front paw. They have four toes on each back paw. Some kittens are born with more toes than normal. They are called polydactyl (pah-lee-DAK-tul), which means "many-toed."

Calico kittens are tricolor. They have orange, white, and black or tabby markings. Almost all calico kittens are female. Only about one calico kitten in 3,000 is male. Male calicos are almost always sterile, which means they cannot make babies.

For example, all pure breed Siamese cats have dark feet and tails and blue eyes. Manx cats all have stubby tails and striped fur. Mixed-breed cats can be all different colors, from orange and white to all black and everything in between.

Whether you get your pet from a shelter or from an ad, you should take it to a veterinarian. The vet will examine the kitten to make sure it is healthy. He or she can also give you more tips for taking care of your kitten.

Cats love the smell of their human friends and will often nap in the bed or on pillows.

PREPARE YOUR HOME

Kittens need a safe and healthy home. You will have to get your house ready for your new pet. Some things you need to think about are a bed, a litter box, food, toys, and safety.

Keeping your kitten safe is your most important job. You will need to kitten-proof your house. Kittens are curious and they like to explore. You must make sure the kitten will not get hurt while it is playing.

Put away all soaps and cleaning supplies. Kittens may try to eat them and could get poisoned. Keep trash covered. Kittens may try to eat trash, and they could choke. They could eat something rotten. Keep your kitten out of trash cans. Don't let your kitten play with electric cords. Kittens will try to chew them. If the cord is plugged in, the kitten could get shocked. The electricity could hurt or kill the kitten. Keep your kitten away from fire. They may try to play with the flame and get burned.

Your kitten will need a safe place to sleep. They like to sleep in closed in spaces, where they can feel safe. You can make a bed from a cardboard box. Make a door for your kitten and put in an old blanket. Place it in a quiet room. Show your kitten the bed and let the kitten play in it. Soon your kitten will like the bed.

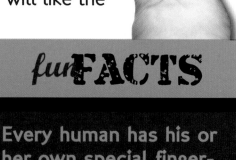

*fun*FACTS

Every human has his or her own special finger-prints. Your fingerprints are different from everyone else's in the world. A cat's nose pad is like a human finger-print. No two nose prints are the same.

You will need special food for your kitten. Do not feed your kitten people food because it can make kittens sick. Buy dry food from the store. Set it out in a bowl, and allow your kitten to eat when it is hungry. Always keep a bowl of fresh water next to its food.

You will need a plastic tub for a litter box. Make sure the sides are low. Kittens have little legs, and low sides make it easy for the kitten to get in and out. Fill the tub partway with cat litter. You can buy cat litter at the store. Most cat litter is clay, but some is made from old newspapers. The clay or paper is in tiny

pieces, so the kitten will be able to dig in it. Your kitten will quickly learn to use the litter box.

Cleaning the litter box is one of the responsibilities of owning a kitten. You should clean it every day. To do this, you will need a scoop with holes in the bottom. Use the scoop to pick up the cat poop. Put the poop in an outside trash can (use a plastic bag if your parents tell you to). Every week you need to empty the entire litter box into the trash can and wash the box. When it is dry, fill it with fresh, clean litter. If you do not clean out the litter box, your kitten will stop using it and will go to the bathroom on your floor. A clean litter box is very important.

Your kitten will need toys. When you are gone your kitten may get bored, but toys will keep her happy. A scratching post is a great idea because kittens like to scratch. You can make a scratching post from an old piece of carpet. Attach it to a board or pole and put it in a box. Your kitten will scratch the carpet on the post and not scratch the furniture.

Kittens like balls and toys that roll. Pull toys are also fun because kittens like to chase them. Be careful to give them toys that are safe and do not break apart. This will keep your kitten from choking. Taking care of a kitten is a lot of fun, but it is also hard work.

Some people are **allergic** (AL-ur-jik) to cats. Cat hair and saliva contain a special protein that can cause humans to sneeze, cough, or itch. If you want a kitten, be sure no one in your family has a cat allergy.

BRINGING YOUR KITTEN HOME

Bringing home a kitten is exciting. You will be happy to play with it, but your kitten may be a little scared. Everything in your house will be new to your kitten. You can help it feel safe and comfortable.

Your kitten will want to see his new home, but don't let it just run around. Keep your kitten in one room and stay with her as she explores. Kittens can get stuck in boxes. They can get lost in closets. You need to watch your kitten all the time.

Make sure your kitten sees the litter box. Keep the litter box away from the kitten's food and water. Kittens like their food in one place, and they want their litter box in another place. Once you have shown the kitten the litter box and food bowls, don't move them. That will confuse your kitten and could cause bathroom mistakes.

Help your kitten meet your family. Kittens can be scared of new people. Let your kitten meet your family one person at a time. Don't invite lots of friends over to see the kitten. Let it get used to your family first. Wait at least a week to have friends visit.

To make your kitten happy, play with it at least two times every day. Play for at least fifteen minutes each time. If kittens are bored, they will tear things up to get attention. It is your job to keep your kitten entertained. Even when a kitten grows up, it will still need playtime with you.

Watch your kitten to learn what it is thinking. If your kitten growls, it may be scared. If it hisses, it may be angry. Petting your kitten will make it feel better. The longer you have your kitten, the better you will understand it.

Kittens will rub against your legs. This shows they are happy. It is also how they mark you with their **scent**. Kittens have glands on their faces. The glands

Kittens show their affection by rubbing their face on people, their pillows, and their blankets. They rub off a scent that marks you as their special person.

are tiny pockets in the skin. They hold a liquid that has a smell. A person cannot smell it, but other kittens can. It tells other kittens that you are your kitten's special person.

Kittens are great pets. They are also a big responsibility. If you want a pet kitten, you will need to talk to your parents. Everyone needs to agree when you adopt a kitten. The kitten will be a part of your family.

You can tell your parents what you have learned from this book. Tell them you know how to take care of a litter box, and you know how to pick out a healthy kitten. Tell them you can keep a kitten safe. Remember that taking care of a kitten is a big job. It is fun. But it is a job you must do every day.

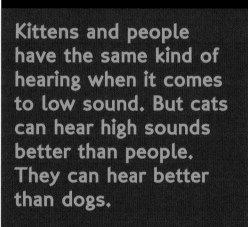

funFACTS

Kittens and people have the same kind of hearing when it comes to low sound. But cats can hear high sounds better than people. They can hear better than dogs.

Tell your parents all you have learned, and you may be able to convince them that you can take care of a pet kitten.

Books

Becker, Marty, D.V.M., and Spadafori. *Why Do Cats Always Land on Their Feet?* Deerfield Beach, Florida: Health Communications, 2006.

Blackaby, Susan, and Charlene Delage. *A Cat for You: Caring for Your Cat.* Mankato, Minnesota: Picture Window Books, 2006.

Choron, Susan, Harry Choron, and Arden Moore. *Planet Cat: A CAT-alog.* New York: Houghton Mifflin, 2007.

Evans, Mark. *Kitten.* New York: DK Children, 1992.

Hotchner, Tracie. *The Cat Bible: Everything Your Cat Expects You to Know.* New York: Penguin Group, 2007.

Phillips, Meredith. *Cat Chat.* Mankato, Minnesota: Compass Point Books, 2004.

Works Consulted

Alderton, David. *Cats (Eyewitness Handbook).* New York: Dorling Kindersley Inc., 1995.

Christensen, Wendy. *Complete Guide to Cat Care.* New York: St. Martin's Press, 2002.

Edney, Andrew. *Complete Cat Care Manual.* New York: Dorling Kindersley, 1995.

Kilcommons, Brian, and Sarah Wilson. *Good Owners, Good Cats.* New York: Warner Books, 1995.

Masson, Jeffrey Moussaieff. *The Nine Emotional Lives of Cats.* New York: Ballantine Books, 2003.

Siegal, Mordecai. *The Cat Fanciers' Association Complete Cat Book.* New York: Harper Collins, 2004.

Web Addresses

Animal Humane Society
www.animalhumanesociety.org/

PBS: Extraordinary Cats
www.pbs.org/wnet/nature/excats/cats.html

Purina: Kitten Care
www.catchow.com/KittenCareCenterHome.aspx

Photo Credits: Cover, p. 19—Rosco Elehman; pp. 4, 10—Happy Endings Animal Rescue; p. 6—Abbey Cat Adoptions; pp. 9, 28—JupiterImages; pp. 13, 16—Marty Colton; pp. 14 (top), 21, 22—CreativeCommons; p. 14 (bottom)—Barbara Marvis; p. 26—FunFreeWalls.com. Every effort has been made to locate all copyright holders of material used in this book. If any errors or omissions have occurred, corrections will be made in future editions of the book.

allergies (AL-ur-jees)—Reactions such as sneezing or coughing that happen when a person is around a usually harmless substance.

feline (FEE-lyn)—An animal that belongs to the cat family, such as a lion, tiger, or and domestic cat.

infection (in-FEK-shen)—An illness that spreads through the body.

kitten (KIT-ten)—A cat that is under one year of age.

litter box (LIH-ter BOKS)—A container in which a kitten uses the toilet.

mammal (MAA-mul)—Any of the warm-blooded animals that have hair and give milk to their young.

neuter (NOO-ter)—To surgically remove a male kitten's reproductive parts.

nocturnal (nok-TUR-nul)—Active at night rather than in the day.

predator (PREH-duh-tur)—An animal that kills other animals for food.

pupil (PYOO-pul)—The dark part at the center of the eye that changes size to let in more or less light.

purr (PUR)—A deep rumbling sound a kitten makes when it is happy or content.

retractable claw (ree-TRAKT-uh-bul KLAW)—One of the pointed, curved nails on the end of the kitten's toes that can be moved in and out of the toe as the kitten decides.

scent (SENT)—The smell that is given off by an animal.

spay (SPAY)—To surgically remove a female kitten's reproductive organs.

veterinarian (veh-truh-NAYR-ee-un)—An animal doctor.

whisker (WIS-ker)—One of the long stiff hairs that grow on each side of a kitten's mouth and over its eyes.